MW00452131

SUNDAY MORNING URGANIST

Alfred's Classic Editions

The seasons of each church year include several special Sundays that focus on the celebration of events in both the Christian church and our nation. This collection provides church organists with a wealth of solos appropriate for those specific occasions (for a list of included occasions, see page two). The musical talents of several well-known arrangers are represented, giving this compilation a variety of musical styles. *Solos for Special Sundays* is the perfect all-in-one resource for the entire church year and will undoubtedly become an essential part of any church organist's repertoire.

TABLE OF CONTENTS (Alphabetical)

Alfred Music Publishing Co., Inc.
P.O. Box 10003
Van Nuys, CA 91410-0003
alfred.com

Copyright © MMIX by Alfred Music Publishing Co., Inc.
All Rights Reserved. Printed in USA.

No part of this book shall be reproduced, arranged, adapted, recorded, publicly performed, stored in a retrieval system, or transmitted by any means without written permission from the publisher. In order to comply with copyright laws, please apply for such written permission and/or license by contacting the publisher at alfred.com/permissions.

ISBN-10: 0-7390-6209-3
ISBN-13: 978-0-7390-6209-8

Cover Image: © istockphoto.com/groveb

TABLE OF CONTENTS (by Event/Season)

COME, THOU LONG-EXPECTED JESUS

SW: Solo Reed 8'
GT: Principals 8', 4', 2', Mixture
PED: Bourdons 16', 8', Gt. to Ped.

Rowland H. Prichard
Arranged by James Pethel

With movement, but not fast

© 2009 ALFRED MUSIC PUBLISHING CO., INC.
All Rights Reserved

O COME, O COME, EMMANUEL

Plainsong, adapted by Thomas Helmore
Arranged by Hal Hopson
Hammond Registrations by Porter Heaps

Pipe Organ Registration

R. H. Solo - Cornet

L. H. Accompaniment - 8' Flute

Sw. (A♯) 00 5777 654

(B) 00 4686 530

Gt. [A♯] 00 5543 220

[B] 44 7857 666

Ped. 33

© 2009 ALFRED MUSIC PUBLISHING CO., INC.
All Rights Reserved

8', 4' Flutes
(and perhaps 8' String)

UKRAINIAN BELL CAROL

SW: Foundations 8', 4', 2', Mixture
GT: Foundations 8', 4', 2', Mixture, Sw. to Gt.
PED: Foundations 16', 8', 4', Sw. and Gt. to Ped.

Traditional Ukrainian Melody
Arranged by Edward L. Good

© 2009 ALFRED MUSIC PUBLISHING CO., INC.
All Rights Reserved

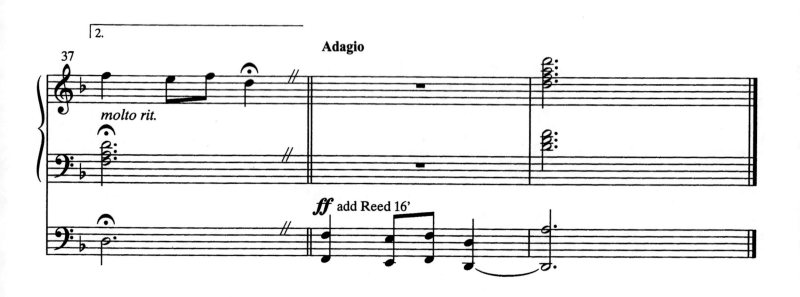

GOOD CHRISTIAN MEN, REJOICE

SW: Flutes 8', 4'
GT: Flutes 8', 4'
CH: Reed 8'
PED: 16', 8'

Traditional German Carol
Arranged by James Pethel

Not too fast, but with a light humor

© 2009 ALFRED MUSIC PUBLISHING CO., INC.
All Rights Reserved

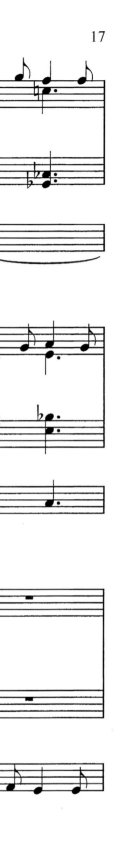

ANGELS WE HAVE HEARD ON HIGH

SW: Celeste 8', Flute 2', trem.
GT: Flutes 8', 2'
CH: String 8', Flute 8'
PED: Sw. to Ped. 8'

Traditional French Carol
Arranged by Keith Chapman

© 2009 ALFRED MUSIC PUBLISHING CO., INC.
All Rights Reserved

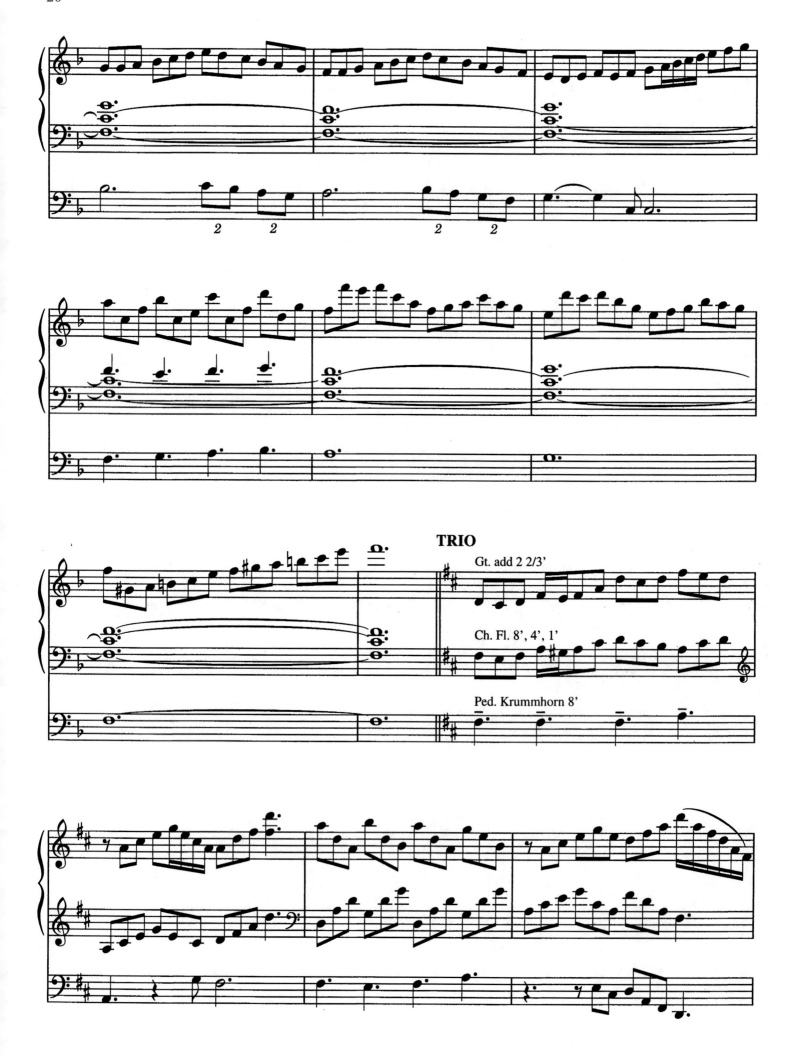

TRIO

Gt. add 2 2/3'

Ch. Fl. 8', 4', 1'

Ped. Krummhorn 8'

Ch. Str. 8', Fl. 8'

off Krum., add Sw. to Ped.

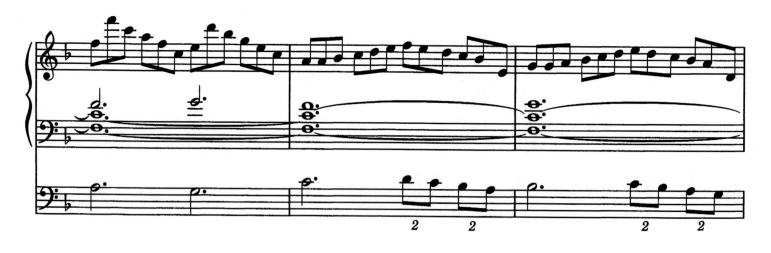

GOOD KING WENCESLAS

I: Krummhorn 8'
II   Flutes 8', 4'
Ped: Soft 16', 8'

Traditional
Arranged by Alfred V. Fedak

Brisk and happy ($\sharp$=88)

© 2009 ALFRED MUSIC PUBLISHING CO., INC.
All Rights Reserved

INFANT HOLY, INFANT LOWLY

SW: Oboe 8'
GT: Flute 8'
CH: String 8', Flute 8'
PED: Sw. to Ped.

Traditional Polish Carol
Arranged by Keith Chapman

© 2009 ALFRED MUSIC PUBLISHING CO., INC.
All Rights Reserved

30

SW: Flutes 8', 4', 2'
GT: Solo Reed 8'
PED: 16', 8', 4'

DING! DONG! MERRILY ON HIGH

Thoinot Arbeau
Arranged by James Pethel

Light and bright, with spirit (♩ = 105)

© 2009 ALFRED MUSIC PUBLISHING CO., INC.
All Rights Reserved

*Optional: Handbell choir may double manuals ad lib. as desired.

AWAY IN A MANGER

William James Kirkpatrick
Arranged by Keith Chapman

SW: Voix Celeste
GT: Ch. and Sw. to Gt.
CH: Unda Maris 8'
PED: Bourdon 16', Ch. to Ped.

© 2009 ALFRED MUSIC PUBLISHING CO., INC.
All Rights Reserved

Slower

pp

, p

Ped. soft Reed 8', Sw. to Ped.

Ped. off Reed, add Bd. 16'

O COME, ALL YE FAITHFUL

I: Solo Trumpet 8', Principal 4'
II: Principals 8', 4', 2', Mixture
PED: Bourdons 16', 8', II to Ped.

John F. Wade
Arranged by David Lasky

© 2009 ALFRED MUSIC PUBLISHING CO., INC.
All Rights Reserved

GOD REST YE MERRY, GENTLEMEN
with THE FIRST NOEL

Old English Carols
Arranged by Lindsay Lafford

© 2009 ALFRED MUSIC PUBLISHING CO., INC.
All Rights Reserved

BRING A TORCH, JEANETTE, ISABELLA

I: Flutes 8', 4', Strings 8', 4'
II: Flute 8', 2 2/3', 1 3/5'
PED: Soft 16', I to Ped.

French Carol
Arranged by Jerry Westenkuehler

© 2009 ALFRED MUSIC PUBLISHING CO., INC.
All Rights Reserved

HARK! THE HERALD ANGELS SING

SW: Flute 8', Voix Celeste
GT: Flutes 8', 4'
PED: Flutes 16', 8'

Felix Mendelssohn
Arranged by Keith Chapman

Moderato

© 2009 ALFRED MUSIC PUBLISHING CO., INC.
All Rights Reserved

O THE DEEP, DEEP LOVE OF JESUS

SW: String Celeste 8'
GT: Flutes 8', 4'
CH: Oboe 8', trem.
PED: Flutes 16', 8', Sw. to Ped.

Thomas J. Williams
Arranged by Jerry Westenkuehler

© 2009 ALFRED MUSIC PUBLISHING CO., INC.
All Rights Reserved

Gradually reduce to Swell String Celeste 8'

p Sw.

Ped. Flutes 16', 8'

add soft 32'

WONDROUS LOVE

SW: Salicional 8', Voix Celeste
GT: Ch. to Gt.
CH: Flute 8'
PED: Bourdon 16', Sw. to Ped.

Southern Harmony, 1835
Arranged by David Maxwell

© 2009 ALFRED MUSIC PUBLISHING CO., INC.
All Rights Reserved

AH, HOLY JESUS

SW: String 8', Flute 8'
PED: Solo Reed 4', (trem.)

Johann Heerman
Arranged by James Pethel

© 2009 ALFRED MUSIC PUBLISHING CO., INC.
All Rights Reserved

*The F may be played with or without the sharp at the discretion of the organist.

O SACRED HEAD, NOW WOUNDED

SW: Flutes 8', 4', 2', Mixture II
GT: Bourdon 8', Flute 4'
PED: Soft 16', 8'

Hans Leo Hessler
Harmonization by Johann Sebastian Bach
Arranged by John G. Barr

© 2009 ALFRED MUSIC PUBLISHING CO., INC.
All Rights Reserved

68

HOSANNA, LOUD HOSANNA

Gesangbuch der Herzogl
Arranged by James Pethel

© 2009 ALFRED MUSIC PUBLISHING CO., INC.
All Rights Reserved

PALM SUNDAY PRELUDE

Melchior Teschner
Arranged by Lindsay Lafford

© 2009 ALFRED MUSIC PUBLISHING CO., INC.
All Rights Reserved

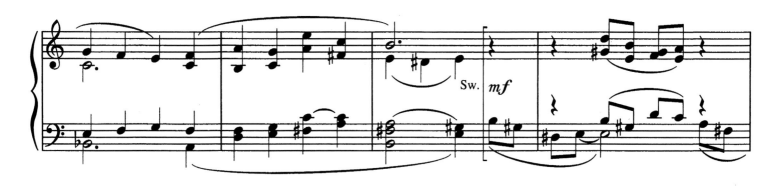

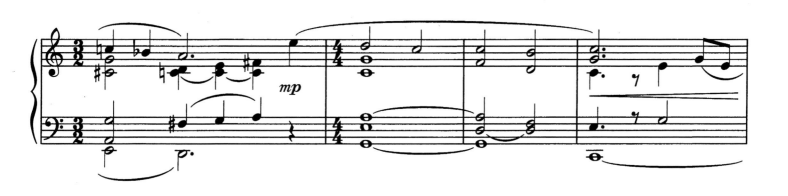

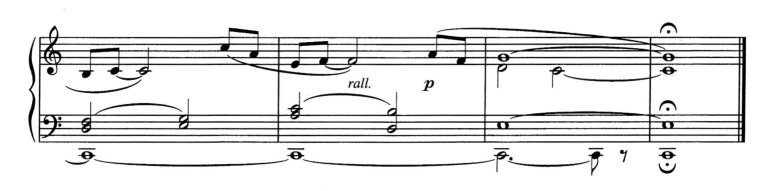

CHRIST THE LORD IS RISEN TODAY

SW: Reeds 8', 4'
GT: Principals 8', 4', 2'
CH: Solo Reed 8'
PED: Principals 16', 8', 4'

Lyra Davidica
Arranged by James Pethel

© 2009 ALFRED MUSIC PUBLISHING CO., INC.
All Rights Reserved

TRUMPET VOLUNTARY ON
"CHRIST THE LORD IS RISEN TODAY"

(With Hymn Tune "Llanfair"*)

SW: Trompette 8', 4'
GT: Principals 8', 4', 2', Mixture
PED Principals 16', 8', 4', Mixture

Lyra Davidica
John G. Barr

*Hymn tune "Llanfair" by Robert Williams, 1817

© 2009 ALFRED MUSIC PUBLISHING CO., INC.
All Rights Reserved

HALLELUJAH CHORUS
(from "Messiah")

SOLO: Trompette en Chamade
SW:
GT: Full without Reeds and Mixtures
CH: all manuals coupled
PED: Full without heavy Reeds

George Frideric Handel
Arranged by Virgil Fox

© 2009 ALFRED MUSIC PUBLISHING CO., INC.
All Rights Reserved

TO ALL THE WORLD

(A Sequence of Hymns on the Christian Mission)
O Zion, Haste / Where Cross the Crowded Ways of Life /
I Love to Tell the Story / Hail to the Brightness

SW: Principals 8', 4', 2'
GT: Principals 8', 4', 2', Sw. to Gt.
PED: 16', Sw. to Ped.

Arranged by Jerry Van Der Pol

© 2009 ALFRED MUSIC PUBLISHING CO., INC.
All Rights Reserved

AMERICA, THE BEAUTIFUL

SW: Full to Mixture
GT: Full to Mixture, Sw. to Gt.
GH: Solo Reed 8'
PED: 16', 8', 4', Sw. & Gt. to Ped.

Samuel A. Ward
Arranged by Matthew H. Corl

© 1996 THE H.W. GRAY CO.
All Rights Controlled and Administered by ALFRED MUSIC PUBLISHING CO., INC.
All Rights Reserved

108

Gt. add Sw. Reed 8'

SW: Soft 8', 4'
CH: Flutes 8', 2'
PED: 16', 8'

*MATERNA - Samuel A. Ward, 1888
**AMERICA - Thesaurus Musicus, 1744

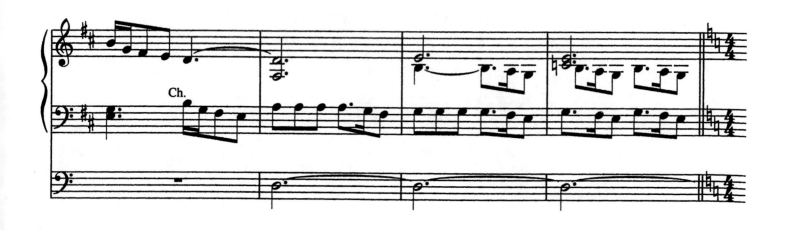

Tempo primo

poco rit.

Ch. Solo Reed

GOD OF OUR FATHERS

SW: Principals 8', 4', Mixture, Reeds 8', 4'
GT: Principals 8', 4', 2', Sw. to Gt.
CH: Solo Reed *ff*
PED: Principals 16', 8', 4', Mixture, Sw. to Ped.

George W. Warren
Arranged by Mark Thewes

© 2009 ALFRED MUSIC PUBLISHING CO., INC.
All Rights Reserved

* Fanfares can be played on same manual, or on **fff** solo reed (an octave lower, if needed.)
This verse is freely adapted from an arrangement heard at the U. S. Naval Academy in Annapolis, Maryland.

HOLY, HOLY, HOLY! LORD GOD ALMIGHTY

SW: Solo Reed 8'
GT: Principals 8', 4', 2'
CH: Flutes 8', 4', 2'
PED: Principals 16', 8', Gt. to Ped.

John B. Dykes
Arranged by James Pethel

© 2009 ALFRED MUSIC PUBLISHING CO., INC.
All Rights Reserved

NOW THANK WE ALL OUR GOD

SW: Full
GT: Full
PED: Full

Johann Crüger
Arranged by James Pethel

© 2009 ALFRED MUSIC PUBLISHING CO., INC.
All Rights Reserved